Parliament Great Britain

Report from the Committee of secrecy appointed by the House of commons

Assembled at Westminster

Parliament Great Britain

Report from the Committee of secrecy appointed by the House of commons
Assembled at Westminster

ISBN/EAN: 9783337150457

Printed in Europe, USA, Canada, Australia, Japan

Cover: Foto ©Suzi / pixelio.de

More available books at **www.hansebooks.com**

REPORT

FROM THE

COMMITTEE OF SECRECY

APPOINTED BY THE

HOUSE OF COMMONS,

Aſſembled at Weſtminſter, in the Sixth Seſſion of the Thirteenth Parliament of

GREAT BRITAIN,

TO ENQUIRE INTO

THE STATE

OF THE

EAST INDIA COMPANY.

LONDON:

PRINTED FOR T. EVANS, AT No. 54, IN PATERNOSTER-ROW.

M. DCC. LXXIII.

REPORT

FROM THE

COMMITTEE OF SECRECY

APPOINTED TO ENQUIRE INTO

THE STATE

OF THE

EAST INDIA COMPANY.

The Committee of Secrecy appointed to enquire into the State of the East India Company, and for that Purpose to inspect the Books and Accounts of the said Company; and to report to the House what they find material therein, in respect to the Debts, Credits and Effects of the Company, as also to the Management and present Situation of the Company's Affairs, together with their Observations thereupon.

HAVING finished their inquiries into the special matters referred to them, by the instruction of the house, of the 30th day of November, proceeded in the next place, in pursuance of the order of the house, to state the debts, credits, and effects of the said company; and as these are dispersed in different parts of the world, they thought it would contribute to a more clear and perfect knowledge of the company's affairs, if they distinguished such of their debts, credits, and effects, as are in England, from such as are now abroad, at their presidencies in India, in China, at Saint Helena, and floating on the sea.

And your committee thought it right, in stating the debts, credits, and effects, of the company in England, to begin by stating an account of the cash in the company's treasury, on the first day of December, 1772, being the day on which they entered on this inquiry, and of such sums as the company expect to avail themselves of, from the produce of their present sale, and of all other sums which they will be entitled to receive, before the 2d day of March 1773, being the day on which their next sale will probably begin; and to state, *per contra*, on the debit side of the account, all demands upon the company in England already due, and such others as will become due before the said 2d day of March, of which day your committee have made choice for the final period to this first part of their state of the Company's affairs in England, as the Company will then have received the principal payments for goods sold in their present sale. And this first account may therefore be properly considered as the cash account of the said Company.

And in the next place, your committee have stated the remainder of the Company's effects and credits in England, and, *per contra*, all other debts of the Company, which will not become due till after the said 2d day of March 1773.

And your committee having thus finished a state of the Company's debts, credits, and effects, in England, they proceeded to state a like account of the debts, credits, and effects, of the Company abroad, at their presidencies in India, in China, at Saint Helena, and floating on the sea.

And

And your committee find, that on the said first day of December 1772, the United Company of Merchants of England trading to the East-Indies, had

	£.	s	d.
Cash in their treasury —	149,169,	15	9
And that the following sums are now due, or will become due, to the said Company, before the said 2d day of March; viz.			
From the Board of Ordnance for Salt Petre —	4,500	—	--
For one quarter's interest, due the 5th of January 1773, From the public on £. 4,200,000 —	31,500	--	--
For expences on the expedition to the Manilha —	28,365	15	8
For goods already sold in the present sale, discount deducted, and deducing 6,000 allowed (per estimate) for private trade in former sales -	1,090,065	--	--
For remainder of goods to be put up at the present sale, payment on which will be due before the said 2d of March 1773 —	285,885	--	--

For

Your committee find that the Company claimed, for their expences on this expedition, by a memorial presented to the Commissioners of his Majesty's Treasury, the 10th of February 1768, the sum of £.168,243 9s 2d. But the Commissioners of the Treasury determined by their minute of the 15th of June, 1770, that the Company were entitled only to the expences incurred antecedent to the surrender of the Island of Manilha to the Company's servants, on the 2d of November 1762: In consequence whereof, an account of such expences was delivered by the Company to the Treasury, on the 19th of October 1770, amounting to the said sum of £.28,365 15s 8d, and by an act 11th of George III, the same is directed to be paid to the said Company, but hath not been yet received by them.

For other goods to be sold, being Bengal, Coast, and Surat piece goods, damaged drugs nankeen, cloth and china ware, discount deducted	54,925	--	--
To profit arising to the company from the private trade imported and sold at their sales, per estimate -	25,000	--	--
	1,669,410,	11	5

And your committee find, that the debts of the said united company of merchants of England trading to the East Indies, which are due on the said 1st day of December, 1772, or which will become due before the said 2d day of March 1773; are as followeth; viz.

	l.	s.	d.			
To his Majesty for customs on unrated goods, due the 5th of Aug 1772 —	203,619	7	7			
Interest thereon from the 5th of August to the 1st of December, at 6 per Cent. per Ann. -	3,916	3	9			
				207,535	11	4
To his majesty, for second moiety for customs on ships arrived in season 1771, which will be payable before and on the 20th of February, 1773 -				15,515,	16	-
To his majesty, for first moiety on several ships arrived in 1772, which will be payable before the said 2d day of March 1773, per estimate - -				50,063	18	-
To his majesty, for unrated customs on September sales 1771, which will be payable on the 27th of January 1773, per estimate - - - -				214,359	-	-
To his majesty, for indemnity on tea, payable the 5th of July 1772, pursuant to an act 12 Geo. III. cap. 7. -	117,314	1	4			

Interest

The profit arifing from private trade falling almoft entirely in the September fale, credit is here given for the year's profit on fuch trade.

Your committee find that the Company have obtained from the Commiffioners of the Treafury, three fucceffive warrants of refpite for this fum; as appears by the papers, hereunto annexed, A. B. C.

Interest from the said 5th of July to the 1st of December 1772, at 12 per cent, per annum -	5,708	4	3			
				123,022	5	7
To his majesty more for indemnity on tea, for the year ended the 5th day of July 1772, payable on 11th of October 1772, pursuant to an act 7 Geo. III. cap. 50. —	84,842	8	8			
Interest on ditto from the said 11th of Oct. to the said 1st of December 1772, at 12 per cent. per annum —	1,394	13	5			
				86,237	2	1
To his majesty for half a year's payment, pursuant to an act 9 Geo. III. cap. 24, which became due on the 1st of February 1772, and was payable on the 29th of September following —	200,000	0	0			
Interest thereupon, from the said 29th day of September to the 1st of December 1772, at 15 per cent. per ann. ——	5,095	17	10			
				205,095	17	10
To the Bank of England for a loan already due -	400,000	0	0			
Interest on ditto from the 17th of September to the said 1st of December, 1772, at 4 per cent. per annum,	3,243	16	9			
				403,243	16	9
To the Bank more for a loan which will be due on the 6th of December 1772 -	100,000	0	0			
Interest on the same from the 6th of October, to the said 1st of December 1772 -	602	14	9			
				100,602	14	9

To

Your

To the Bank of England, for interest from the 6th of August 1772 to the said 1st of December following on 100,000l. borrowed on bond, at 4 per cent. per annum, as per agreement with the Bank -	1,271	4	8

To bills of exchange, payable before the 2d of March 1773, interest included -	30,127	1	7
To ditto past due, and not presented for payment, interest included -	8,241	--	--
To freight and demorrage to the 1st of December 1772, with interest then due on the several balances, at 4 per cent. per annum -	276,307	15	6
To ditto that will become due on or before the 2d day of March 1773 -	115,849	5	-

Your committee find that the East-India Company have been accustomed to borrow these loans of the Bank, from 2 months to 2 months; and Mr Tookey, the deputy accomptant of the East-India company, informed your committee, that, as far as his knowledge goes, these loans have hitherto been discharged out of the produce of the sales that were making at the time of borrowing the same. No part of the present loan was discharged in this manner, though the directors of the Bank have frequently solicited the payment thereof: Besides these loans, the company borrowed of the Bank £ 100,000 on bond, on the 6th day of August 1772, which your committee intend to state as part of the bond debt of the said company: But as the company by agreement pay on this debt the same interest they pay on their other loans to the Bank, your committee have thought it right to state the interest on the same specially, in this part of the account.

Your committee find by Mr Richard Cole, freight accomptant to the said company, that they have not paid any freight on their ships arrived in season 1772, except wages: And that there are balances due on 28 ships that arrived in 1771, to the amount of from £.2000 to £.5000 each ship. If the company do not pay their balances at the end of 12 months after the ships are cleared, such balances run at 4 *per cent, per annum* interest. And Mr Cole informed your committee, that there have been instances when the company have been more backward in these payments; but in general it has not been the case.

Your

	£.	s.	d.
To wages and first advances to be paid to 3 ships expected, viz. the Godfrey, Colebroke, and Pigot, per estimate	30,000	--	--
To arrears of dividends on stock to the 5th of January 1772 —	21,966	17	—
To arrears of interest on bonds to the 30th of April 1772 —	22,486	4	7
To arrears of interest on annuities to the 5th of April 1772 —	11,830	1	9
To dividends on stock, due the 5th of July 1772, for the half year preceding, and remaining unpaid —	5,891	—	—
To interest on bonds, due the 30th of September 1772, for the half year preceding, remaining unpaid -	6,783	—	—
To interest on annuities, due the 10th of October 1772, for the half year preceding, remaining unpaid -	12,631	—	—
For warrants passed the court of directors, unpaid - -	10,900	—	—
For commissions to supra cargoes already due, per estimate - -	29,000	—	o
For payments in the department of the committee of shipping, due before the 2d of March 1773 - -	36,840	—	—
For the like in the department of the committee of buying - -	58,035	—	—
For silver for exportation - -	40,000	—	—
For indemnity on teas, to be paid the buyers before the 2d of March 1773, for 1 sh. per lib. Excise on teas taken out for home consumption, and for drawbacks on teas taken out for exportation, according to agreement made with the buyers, per estimate -	30,000	—	—
For charges of merchandize to the 2d of March 1772, per estimate -	30,000	—	—
	2,183,835	12	5

Which

Your committee having been assured that these 3 ships are expected to arrive in this season, they thought it right to state in this account such payments as will probably be made on account of the said ships, before the 2d of March 1773; and they will credit the company with their cargoes under the article of goods in warehouse in England on the said 2d of March 1773.

As all these arrears are already due, and must be paid, if demanded, your committee thought it right to state them in this part of the account, though some of them are of old standing, and may probably never be demanded.

Your committee find that the company have, for the most part, regularly paid their debts under these two articles, and are not now more than usual in arrear.

Which first sum of £.1,669,410 11s 5d being the amount of cash in the company's treasury on the 1st day of December 1772, and of such sums as the company will be intitled to receive, before the 2d day of March 1773, being deducted from the sum of £.2,183,835 12s 5d which is the amount of the debts of the said company, which are due on the said 1st day of December, or which will become due before the said 2d day of March 1773; your committee find that the balance against the company on the said 2d day of March, for debts that will then be due, is the sum of £.514,425 1s.

Your committee think it right to observe, that in the above account they have calculated the interest on the several debts of the company, bearing interest to the 1st day of December 1772, being the day from which the above account commences, except on bills of exchange, on each of which they have calculated the interest to the day on which such bill becomes payable: The interest on the other debts will continue till such time as the debt, on which it is payable, is discharged. As it was impossible for your committee to ascertain when the company will discharge every particular debt, the interest could not be otherwise calculated: But your committee think it right to observe, that the debts of the company, bearing interest on the said 1st day of December 1772, at the different rates of 3, 4, 6, 12, and 15 *per cent.* amount to no less a sum than £2,093,978 2s 5d as appears by the account hereunto annexed, besides what they owe to their annuitants and bondholders, which will be stated hereafter.

Your committee proceeded in the next place to state the remainder of the company's effects and credits in England, and such of their debts as will not become due till after the 2d day of March 1773.

And

And they find that there is due from the public to the company, in consequence of several sums advanced by them, pursuant to the acts 9 and 10 W. III. 6 Queen Anne, and 17 Geo. II. - -	4,200,000	—	—
And that the value of their goods in their warehouses in England, which will remain unsold on the 2d March 1773, by ships already arrived; discount, customs, and commission to supra cargoes thereon deducted: is per estimate -	2,860,544	—	—
And that the value of the cargoes in the 3 ships, Godfrey, Colebroke, and Pigot, expected to arrive before the said 2d of March 1773, discount and customs thereon deducted, is per estimate - - -	220,450	—	—
And that the value of bullion then remaining in the company's treasury, and paid for, is - -	353	17	9
And that the value of the company's house and warehouses is -	224,919	—	—
And that the value of the ships and vessels belonging to the company, with their stores, is - -	17,735	6	8

And

Your committee find that nearly three-fourths of the value of the goods remaining in the warehouſes is tea, being in wt. 16,811,391lb. which is ſuppoſed to be almoſt ſufficient for three years conſumption. The remainder of the goods in the warehouſe, are piece goods and raw ſilk from Bengal, ſalt-petre, &c. which latter articles will be put up in the next year's ſales.

Mr Tookey, the deputy accomptant, informed your committee, that in this eſtimate is included only the price of the lands and houſes bought, and of the buildings erected; and that no annual repairs are included therein: The repairs of the houſe being carried to the account of charges general; and the repairs of the warehouſes to the account of charges of merchandize. And the company's ſurveyor informed your committee, that on the neareſt calculation he can make on the company's freehold buildings and grounds in London, including the Eaſt-India Houſe, the value of them is £228,000, and that whilſt the trade of the company exiſts, and they can fill their warehouſes, he apprehends they are worth that ſum at 10 *per cent.*

Your committee find, by the examination of Mr Oliver, the maſter attendant of the company's ſhips, that the value of the ſhips, veſſels, &c. as ſtated in his account, is according to the prime

coſt;

And that the company claim, as due from France, for the subsistence and charges of French prisoners during the last war, as per account delivered to Mr secretary Conway, the 16th of November 1765 - -	260,687	8	5
	7,784,689	12	10

Your committee find in the annual account of the Company, a claim on the public for hospital expences for his Majesty's troops on the coast of Coromandel, in the last war; an account of which was delivered to the Commissioners of the Treasury the 12th of June 1770; but it appears by a minute of the Treasury Board of the 29th day of January 1771, that Colonel Monson having then been examined on the subject of the said account, informed the Board, that it was always understood by himself, and others commanding his Majesty's troops serving in India, that the extraordinary expences of the said troops, including the charge of hospitals, were to be paid by the Company; and that the said hospitals were under the management of the officers of the Company, and his Majesty's officers were not permitted to interfere in any wise therein. —And that the Board of Treasury, in consideration of what was alledged by Colonel Monson, determined that they did not think themselves justified in proceeding to the further liquidation of this account, until the Company should have laid before the Board the authorities on which they founded this demand on the public; and it does not appear to your committee that any further proceeding has been had thereon.

And your committee find, that besides the balance due by the company on the 2d of March 1773, for debts become due before the said 2d day of March, being the sum of - -	514,425	1	—

coſt ; but that the real value to the company ſhould be eſtimated at one-third leſs, at which value your committee have ſtated them on the other ſide.

It appears to your committee that this matter is now under conſideration ; but that the Court of France have not yet engaged to pay any part of this ſum.

The company are further indebted,

To the persons who subscribed their bonds in pursuance of an act, passed 23 Geo. II. for annuities, now bearing an interest at the rate of 3 per cent. per annum . -	2,992,440	5	—
And to the holders of their bonds	2,998,124	10	—

And that they are indebted to his majesty, for half a year's payment on £.400,000 per annum, pursuant to an act, 9 Geo. III. cap. 24. which became due on the 1st of August 1772, and will be payable on the 25th of March 1773 - -	200,000	—	—

Your committee find that the Company pay interest after the rate of 3 per cent. per annum, on £. 2,895,107. 10s. of this sum.—And that for £. 100,000. lent by the Bank on bond, they pay the like interest as on their other loans from the Bank; and that the remaining sum, being £. 3,017 bears no interest, as the holders of the bonds for that sum never brought them in to be marked, pursuant to the orders of the General Courts for the reduction of interest.

Your committee observe that so much of this sum as becomes due in respect of the time intervening between the 5th of July and the 1st of August, is subject to an alteration according to the rule laid down by an Act passed in the 9th year of his present Majesty, which provides that if the said Company shall for and during any time or times within the term of 5 years, to be computed from the 1st day of February 1769, reduce the dividends upon their stock, then and in every such case, there shall, for and during the time or times respectively of every such reduction or reductions, be deducted from the said sum of £. 400,000, a sum or sums equal to the amount of each and every such reduction; and if at any time or times within the said term of 5 years the said Company shall reduce the dividends upon their stock to or under the Rate of £. 6 per centum per annum, then in every such case during the respective continuance of every such reduction, the said company shall be, and are thereby, discharged from the payment of the said sum of £. 400,000 or such part thereof as would have become due to the public during the continuance of such reduction.

This

And for cuſtoms for goods ſold before the 2d day of March 1773, but not payable till afterwards; viz. for the ſecond moiety per Ponſborne, Aſia, and Speke, from Bengal -	57,366	9	8
For ſecond moiety per Dutton, and firſt and ſecond per Hampſhire, from Bombay - - -	1,268	18	2
For firſt and ſecond moiety, per Lord North, and Lord Holland, from Fort St. George - -	51,303	15	9
For ſecond moiety on 15 China ſhips, and firſt and ſecond on 5 China ſhips - - -	2,299	16	4
For unrated cuſtoms on March ſales 1772, payable the 18th of Auguſt 1773 - - -	182,823	—	—
For ditto on September ſale 1772, payable in January 1774 - -	184,594	—	—
To 15 per cent. cuſtoms on September ſale 1772, payable the 18th of March 1773 - - -	112,489	—	—
To the bank of England, on account of bullion bought of them -	200,000	—	—

To Bills of Exchange already accepted, and which will become due after the 2d of March 1773, and before the 2d of March 1774, intereſt included	686,150	8	—
For bills of exchange already accepted, and which will become due from the 2d of March 1774, to the 2d of March 1775, intereſt included — —	411,528	9	6
For bills of exchange already accepted, which will become due in the remainder of the year 1775, intereſt included — — —	2,583	3	1

For

This debt bears an interest at 4 per cent. per annum, payable the 19th of October and 19th of April, in every year, and is the Remainder of a debt of £. 736,250, contracted in the years 1756 and 1757, for bullion then bought of the Bank, which by subsequent payments has been reduced to the present sum.

Your committee find by the evidence of Mr. Tookey and Mr. Holt, that these include bills from China as well as from India. The general rule from June 1769 has been to draw at 365 days after sight: the Company give their servants permission to draw bills to a certain amount; some of the bills payable in 1773, are a part of that permission: all the bills from Bengal which were accepted in 1771, were drawn contrary to orders with respect to interest, and part of them with respect to exchange; they were nevertheless accepted on the terms on which they were drawn. Those from Bombay were drawn contrary to orders with

For ſundry payments in the department of the committee of ſhipping for exports, including recruits, for the remainder of the preſent ſeaſon — —	177,105 — —
For ſundry payments in the department of the committee of buying, for the remainder of the ſeaſon — —	101,673 — —
For freight and demorage on ſhips already arrived, payable after the 2d of March 1773 — — —	159,343 — —
For freight and demorage on the ſhips expected to arrive; viz. Godfrey, Colebrooke, and Pigot, payable after the 2d of March 1773, per eſtimate -	18,000 — —
For commiſſion to ſupra cargoes, which will be owing the 2d of March 1773, for goods ſold before that day, but not payable till afterwards —	24,283 — —
To caſh to be paid to the buyers of tea, in lieu of the 1 ſh. per lib. exciſe on teas for home conſumption, and of the drawback on ſuch as ſhall be exported, purſuant to agreement between the Eaſt India Company and the buyers, for tea ſold from March ſale 1767, to the September ſale 1771, both incluſive, and remaining in the warehouſe upon the 2d of March 1773, per eſtimate — —	133,000 — —
To their alms-houſes at Poplar, due the 1ſt of December 1772, and on which is allowed 4 per cent. per annum intereſt — — —	8,313 16 —
	9,219,114 12 6

And the ſum of £. 7,784,689. 12 *s.* 10*d.* being the value of the Company's effects and credits in England, after the 2d day of March 1773, being deducted from the ſum of £. 9,219,114. 12*s.* 6*d.* which conſiſts of the balance due by the Company on the ſaid 2d day of March 1773, for debts become due before and on that day, and of the amount of their debts which will not become due till after the ſaid 2d day of March; your committee find, That the balance againſt the Company, with

with reſpect to intereſt, and part with reſpect to exchange: the terms of part of theſe bills were altered, with reſpect to intereſt, with conſent of the holders.

with reſpect to their debts, credits, and effects, in England, is the ſum of £. 1,434,424. 19s. 8d.

Your committee having thus finiſhed a ſtate of the Company's debts, credits, and effects, in England, proceeded to ſtate a like account of the debts, credits, and effects, of the Company abroad, at their Preſidencies, in China, at Saint Helena, and floating on the ſea.

And your committee find that there is caſh in the ſeveral treaſuries of the Company's preſidencies, and their ſubordinates, *viz.*

		C Rs		s. d.	£.	
Bengal, taken the 31ſt March 1772		7,109,244	at	2 3	799,789	
Fort St. George, Do 20 March 1772	Pags	251,661	at	8	100,664	
Bombay, — Do 17 March 1772	Rupees	393,938	at	2 6	49,242	
Bencoolen — Do 31 Janry 1771	Sp. Dols	173,400	at	5 0	43,350	
						993,045 — —

Caſh at Canton in China, taken the 7th of March 1772; viz. ſilver that will be in the treaſury there, when the bohea unpack'd, the ſouchongs and congous which are to be received, ſhall be paid for, and all balances paid and received, tales 120,534, at 6 s. 8d.		40,178 — —
Caſh at Saint Helena, taken the 30th September 1771		8,852 — —
And that the value of the goods at Bengal, taken 31ſt March 1772, is	£.	
Goods for Europe —	109,813	
Goods for ſale —	128,960	
		238,773 — —
And that the value of their goods at Fort Saint George, taken 20th March 1772, is	£.	
Goods for Europe —	132,184	
Goods for ſale —	93,049	
		225,233 — —

And

This account is the laſt that has been received.

Your committee find by the evidence of Mr. Hoole, auditor of the India accounts, that the goods for Europe are goods of the country actually in their warehouſes, and valued according to what they coſt there: and that the goods for ſale are European goods, ſuch as broad cloth, copper, and lead; and are valued at the prime coſt in Europe, with 10 per cent. advance on the invoice, according to cuſtom, and were actually in their warehouſes when the laſt ſhips came away.

Mr. Hoole gave the ſame evidence with reſpect to theſe goods, as with reſpect to thoſe at Bengal.

The

And that the value of their goods at Bombay, taken the 17th of March 1772 is

	£.	
Goods for Europe —	262,988	
Goods for ſale — —	81,442	
		344,430 — —

And that the Value of their Goods at Bencoolen, taken 31 of January 1771, is,

Goods for Europe — —	8,394 — —

And that the value of their goods in China, taken the 7th of March 1772, is, tales 325,164, at 6s. 8d. each—	108,388 — —

And that there is owing to the Eaſt India Company at their ſeveral preſidencies, as follows; viz.

	£.	
At Bengal and Subordinates 31 March 1772	836,283 — —	
From which deducting for bad debts, according to the obſervations on the other ſide — —	24,710 — —	
The remainder is —		811,573 — —

At

The laſt account of quick ſtock from Bombay, makes the value of the goods from Europe to amount to £. 295,429. but your committee find from the evidence of Mr. Hoole, that the Cargo of the Godfrey, expected ſoon to arrive, eſtimated at £.32,441. is included in this quick ſtock; your committee have therefore deducted it from the above ſum, and ſtated it as on the other ſide.

Mr. Hole gave the ſame evidence in every reſpect with regard to the goods at Bombay, as he did with regard to thoſe at Bengal and Fort Saint George; and added, that the reaſon of the quantity of goods at Bombay being ſo much larger than at the other preſidencies, is, that this account includes the company's goods in Perſia, and at Surat, which are very conſiderable.

Mr. Hoole gave the ſame evidence with reſpect to the goods at Bencoolen, as he did with reſpect to thoſe at Bengal and Fort Saint George.

Your Committee find, by the evidence of Mr. Hoole, that this debt conſiſts of advances made for inveſtments to the agents, factors, and country merchants, and of money owing to the company for goods ſold, to the amount of £433,115. Theſe in general are real advances and debts, and not of long ſtanding.

Mr

At Fort St. George 20th of March, 1772 - - 879,227 --

Mr. Hoole thinks that at Patna and Coſſimbuzar there may be about £.20,000 of old and doubtful debts. Another part of this debt, to the amount of £.105,980. conſiſts of balances due from the company's officers, ſuch as the cuſtom maſter, who collects the company's cuſtoms, the collector of their land revenues, excluſive of the dewanny, and the company's ſteward: and he eſteems this to be a good debt. Another part of this debt, to the amount of £.272,478. conſiſts of balances due from the renters of the dewanny, in the ſeveral diſtricts of the province of Bengal: this balance is ſtruck the 30th of April 1771, and is the balance of the year ended on that day. Mr. Hoole informed your Committee, that the company's ſervants had propoſed to the court of directors to write off ſixteen Lack and 83,876 of Sicca Rupees, being the balance of the preceding year, and which he has therefore not included in this account: and he ſuppoſes that the company's ſervants in Bengal ſtill conſider this arrear of £.272,478. as a debt to be recovered.

In the account delivered to your Committee there was an article of £.19,744. which appears to your Committee, by the evidence of Mr. Hoole, to conſiſt of ſums advanced to contractors and workmen for works and buildings, which will be diſcharged by the performance of their contracts, and ſhould not therefore be conſidered as a debt: and alſo another ſum of £.4,966. which conſiſts of debts from ſeveral people, and the ſame having not varied for ſeveral years, muſt be conſidered as bad debts; your Committee hath therefore not allowed them in this account.

Your Committee find, by the evidence of Mr. Hoole, that this debt conſiſts of advances made for inveſtments, and for money owing for goods ſold to the amount of £.64,942. that this debt is con-

At Bombay 17th March 1772 —				289,792	0	0
From which, deducting for a bad debt, according to the observations on the other side ——	1,665	0	0			
The remainder will be ——				288,127	0	0

An

tinually fluctuating, but he esteems it a good debt: and that another part of this debt, being £.20,820 is owing by the chief of Masulipatam, for bills in his hands, given by the company's farmers and renters for the revenues; and Mr. Hoole thinks this a good debt: and that another part of this debt, being £.13,590. is due by the company's custom master for the balance of sea customs; and he thinks this a good debt: and that another part of this debt, being £.580,609. consists of a balance due from Mahomed Ally Cawn, Nabob of Arcot, part of which sum, being £.180,609. is the balance of his account for general charges defrayed for him, and is good, being part of a debt which he regularly liquidates; the remainder of the said sum of £.580,609. being ten lack of Pagodas, or £.400,000. is a sum carried to his account by the company here towardsthe expence of the war with Heydar Ally. And your Committee find by a letter from the said Nabob Mahomed Ally Cawn, to the court of directors, dated the 20th March 1772, that he engages to discharge this debt, as appears by the letter hereunto annexed. The remainder of this debt, being £.199,266. consists of balances due from the renters and farmers of lands and farms at Fort St. George, and subordinates, which balances are not of long standing, and the present arrear is less than formerly.

Your Committee find, by the evidence of Mr. Hoole, that part of this debt, to the amount of £.111,961. consists of advances for investments, and of money owing to the company for goods sold, and that it is not a debt of long standing: and that another part of the said debt, amounting to £.134,998. consists of money due from the managers of the Bank at Bombay, which Bank is chiefly under the direction of the governor and

For the cargoes of 25 ſhips ſent, and to be ſent out in this ſeaſon, valued at prime coſt here, bullion and every thing included — —		494,597 0 0
For impreſts to owners of ſhips; viz.		
For 5 ſhips in 1770 -	6,237 10 0	
26 ſhips in 1771 -	32,435 0 0	
25 ſhips in 1772 -	31,187 10 0	
		69,860 0 0
For Madeira wines ſent out in 1771, and paid for — —	13,173 0 0	
For 1-3d of wine to be taken in 1772, ditto	3,743 0 0	
		16,916 0 0

And

not included in their account of quick ſtock at Bombay.

And it appears, by the evidence of Mr. Hoole, that none of the ſhips of the ſeaſon 1771, were arrived when the ſaid accounts came away---and that in general every ſhip which arrives in England from India, brings with her (according to orders from the court of directors) an account of the quick ſtock of the company, as it ſtood at the time of her departure from India, in the ſettlement from whence ſhe comes, excluſive of the cargoe ſhe has on board; and that the laſt ſhips which arrived, brought ſuch account from each reſpective preſidency, but that the cargoe of the Colebrooke, tho' not yet arrived, is not included in the quick ſtock at Bengal, as ſhe was laden, when the Clive, the ſhip that brought the account, came away; her cargoe is therefore ſtated as of a ſhip actually arrived, and in the warehouſe here.

For the cargoes of 25 ſhips ſent, and to be ſent out in this ſeaſon, valued at prime coſt here, bullion and every thing included — —				494,597	0	0
For impreſts to owners of ſhips; viz.						
For 5 ſhips in 1770 -	6,237	10	0			
26 ſhips in 1771 -	32,435	0	0			
25 ſhips in 1772 -	31,187	10	0			
				69,860	0	0
For Madeira wines ſent out in 1771, and paid for — —	13,173	0	0			
For 1-3d of wine to be taken in 1772, ditto	3,743	0	0			
				16,916	0	0

And

not included in their account of quick ſtock at Bombay.

And it appears, by the evidence of Mr. Hoole, that none of the ſhips of the ſeaſon 1771, were arrived when the ſaid accounts came away---and that in general every ſhip which arrives in England from India, brings with her (according to orders from the court of directors) an account of the quick ſtock of the company, as it ſtood at the time of her departure from India, in the ſettlement from whence ſhe comes, excluſive of the cargoe ſhe has on board; and that the laſt ſhips which arrived, brought ſuch account from each reſpective preſidency, but that the cargoe of the Colebrooke, tho' not yet arrived, is not included in the quick ſtock at Bengal, as ſhe was laden, when the Clive, the ſhip that brought the account, came away; her cargoe is therefore ſtated as of a ſhip actually arrived, and in the warehouſe here.

And your Committee find that the Company's dead ftock abroad, at their prefidencies in China, at St. Helena, and floating on the fea, is as followeth; viz.

The value of their ftores at Bengal, taken 31 March, 1772, is,

Civil ftores —	— 84,681	0	0			
Military ditto	— 192,726	0	0			
				277,407	0	0

And that the value of their ftores at Fort St. George, taken the 20th of March, 1772, is

Civil ftores —	42,527	0	0			
Military ftores —	224,439	0	0			
				266,966	0	0

And

Mr. Hoole having informed your Committee that theſe ſtores in general are not deſigned for ſale, they have thought it right to ſtate them as part of the dead ſtock of the company abroad: and by the ſame evidence your Committee find that the civil ſtores at Bengal conſiſts of naval ſtores, ſuch as cordage, pitch, tar, and canvas, ſtationary for the factory, and European goods for the uſe of the factory; and that what is here charged is an eſtimate of what was actually there on the 31ſt of March 1772, and is a very perfect valuation according to the European prices---and that the military ſtores at Bengal conſiſt of muſquets, and all other ſtores of a military nature, actually in magazine there, excluſive of thoſe out in ſervice. He thinks that neither the value of guns on the ramparts, nor any other ordnance, is included in this account---and that all in general are valued according to the European prices.

A

Mr. Hoole gave the ſame evidence with reſpect to theſe ſtores as he did with reſpect to thoſe at Bengal, except that the guns on the ramparts are included in this account.

Mr.

And that the value of their ſtores at Bombay, taken the 17th of March, 1772, is,

		£.	s.	d.			
Civil ſtores	—	55,110	0	0			
Military ditto	—	78,515	0	0			
					133,625	0	0

And that the value of their ſtores at Bencoolen, taken the 31ſt January, 1771, is,

		£.	s.	d.			
Civil ſtores	—	42,432	0	0			
Military ditto	—	7,784	0	0			
					50,216	0	0

And that the value of their ſtores at St. Helena, taken the 30th September, 1771, is

		£.	s.	d.			
Civil ſtores	—	20,293	0	0			
Military ſtores	—	17,265	0	0			
					37,558	0	0

And that the value of their ſhips and Veſſels in India, is,

		£.	s.	d.			
At Bengal	——	65,637	0	0			
Fort St. George	—	28,654	0	0			
Bombay	——	74,831	0	0			
Bencoolen	——	12,363	0	0			
					181,485,	0	0

And that the value of their elephants, horſes, camels, and cattle, in India, is,

		£.	s.	d.			
At Bengal	——	38,719	0	0			
Fort St. George	—	17,492	0	0			
Bombay	——	1,098	0	0			
Bencoolen	——	252	0	0			
					57,561	0	0

And

Mr. Hoole again gave the ſame evidence with reſpect to the ſtores at Bombay and Bencoolen, as he did with reſpect to thoſe at Bengal; and he is certain that the guns on the ramparts are not included in the value of the military ſtores of theſe preſidencies.

Mr. Hoole gave the ſame evidence with reſpect to theſe ſtores, as he did with reſpect to thoſe at Bengal, except that the guns on the ramparts are included.

Mr.

And that the value of the plate, household furniture, &c. of the company in India, is,

	£.	s.	d.	£.	s.	d.
At Bengal ———	14,869	0	0			
Fort St. George —	9,019	0	0			
Bombay ———	15,037	0	0			
Bencoolen ———	1,219	0	0			
				40,144	0	0

And that the value of the Company's Plantations, is,

	£.	s.	d.	£.	s.	d.
At Bombay —	29,058	0	0			
St. Helena, including lands and cattle -	11,166	0	0			
				40,224	0	0

And that the value of the Company's Slaves, is,

	£.	s.	d.	£.	s.	d.
At Bombay ———	196	0	0			
Bencoolen ———	14,197	0	0			
St. Helena ———	4,595	0	0			
				18,988	0	0
				6,397,299	10	6

Your Committee find, by the evidence of Mr. Hoole, that the company's veſſels in India are valued according to the prime coſt there, and that at Fort St. George, not only the value of the prime coſt of the veſſels is included, but alſo of all the ſtores that have been ſupplied to them, which has ſometimes made the value of a veſſel amount to double the prime coſt of her building.

That the value of the elephants, horſes, camels, and cattle, is the prime coſt of them there.

That the value of the plate, houſhold furniture, and neceſſaries, is what the company's ſervants paid for them there.

And that the value of the plantations and ſlaves is an eſtimate.

And Mr. Hoole being aſked, whether he could not give a more perfect valuation of theſe effects; he anſwered, that they had no other return made but theſe accounts.

Your

And your Committee find, that the debts of the Company abroad at their presidencies in China, and at St. Helena, are as followeth; viz.

Debts owing by the Company at Bengal — —	1,754,506	0	0
Debts owing by the Company at Fort St. George — —	48,164	0	0
Debts owing by the Company at Bombay — —	213,418	0	0

Debts

Your Committee find, by the evidence of Mr. Hoole, that part of the ſaid debt, being £.1,138,515, is due on bond, and bears an intereſt after the rate of 8 per cent. per annum—And that another part of this debt, being £.130,453. is a fund eſtabliſhed for the ſupport of decayed and diſabled officers and ſoldiers, for which ſum no intereſt is paid in Bengal, but in conſideration thereof, and by agreement made between the company and the Right Hon. Lord Clive, the company pay in England £.9,172. 13*s.* 4*d.* per annum—And that another part of this debt, being £.459,005. is owing to the Mogul, the Nabob, and to his miniſters in part of their tribute and ſtipends; and was due the 10th of November 1771—And that another part of this debt, being £.17,607. conſiſts of ſums, being the eſtates of deceaſed perſons and other depoſits in truſt, paid into the company's treaſury, by order of the mayor's court at Calcutta—And the remainder, being £.8,926. conſiſts of ſeveral ſmall debts owing by the company.

Your Committee find, by the evidence of Mr. Hoole, that part of this debt, being £.29,918. is money borrowed on bond, bearing intereſt at the rate of 8 per cent. per annum—And that another part of this debt, being £. 8,480. is a depoſit of the French jeſuits, and bears an intereſt at the rate of 6 per cent. per annum—And that the remaining ſum of £.9,766. are debts due to ſundry perſons, bearing no intereſt.

Your Committee find, by the evidence of Mr. Hoole, that part of this debt, being £.88,438. is money borrowed on bond, part whereof bears an intereſt at £.9, per cent. per annum, and part at £.10 per cent. per annum—And that another part of the ſaid debt, being £.110,978. is money due

to

Debts owing by the Company at Bencoolen —— ——	16,218	0	0
	2,032,306	0	0

Which ſum of £.2,032,306. being the amount of the debts of the company abroad, being deducted from the ſum of £.6,397,299. 10*s.* 6*d.* being the value of the company's credits and effects abroad, at their preſidencies, in China, at St. Helena, and floating on the ſea—Your Committee find, That the balance in favour of the company abroad, will be £.4,364,993. 10*s.* 6*d.*

	£.	s.	d.
Balance againſt the company on the 1ſt account, being their caſh account, made up to the 2d day of March 1773 —— ——	514,425	1	0
Balance againſt the company on the 2d account, being an account of their debts, including the balance againſt them on their caſh account, and of their effects and credits in England, after the 2d day of March 1773 —— —— —	1,434,424	19	8
Balance in favour of the company on the 3d account, being an account of their debts, credits, and effects abroad, at their preſidencies, in China, at St. Helena, and floating on the ſea — — —	4,364,993	10	6

Your

to the bank at Bombay, and bears no intereſt— And that another part of this debt, being £.5,319, is a ſum conſiſting of the effects of deceaſed perſons, and depoſits in truſt, paid into the company's treaſury, by order of the mayor's court at Bombay; and the remaining ſum of £.8,683. conſiſts of ſmall debts due to ſundry perſons.

Your Committee find, by the evidence of Mr. Hoole, that this ſum is due to ſundry perſons for goods.

Your Committee have not included in the above account, any valuation of the fortifications and buildings of the company abroad.—They are far from thinking that the same ought not to be considered as of great use and value to the company in carrying on their commerce, and protecting their several settlements; but they can by no means agree in opinion with the Court of Directors, who, by their minutes of the 27th of April 1769, ordered, "That the amount of the fortifications, &c. "should again be added to the annual settlement, "to be made up in June 1769." And your Committee find, that such amount was added to the said account, made up in June 1769, and has been added in all the annual accounts made up since that period; and that in the last annual account made up on the 1st of July 1772, there is included, in consequence of such order of the Court of Directors, under the article of factory at Bengal, the sum of 191 lack and 54,558 current rupees, which, at 2*s*. 3*d*. each, amount to the sum of £.2,154,888. which sum, by a memorandum at the foot of the said account, is stated to be the amount of what had been then expended for fortifications, buildings, &c. at Bengal.

Your Committee having no rule by which they can form any judgment of the real value of this part of the company's effects, can only state to the House what they find in the company's books and accounts concerning them: And it appears to your Committee, that in all the annual accompts from the year 1732, which is the first year in which any annual sum was made up, the sum of £.400,000. has been charged under the head of dead stock, which appears to your Committee to be for the dead stock abroad only, as there is another article charged in every such annual account for East India house,

houſe and warehouſes, to the amount of from £.25,000 to £.40,000.

Your Committee find that in the annual account 1765, £.300,000 was deducted from the quick ſtock account of Fort William.

And that in the annual account 1766, the ſaid ſum of £.300,000, together with £.30,000 more, was deducted from the quick ſtock account of Fort William.

And that in the annual account 1767, the ſame ſum of £.330,000 was deducted from the quick ſtock account of Fort William.

And that in the annual account 1768, the ſum of £.860,065, which includes the ſaid ſum of £.330,000 above mentioned, was deducted from the quick ſtock account of Fort William.

And your Committee find, that in the general letter of the court of directors, dated the 16th of March 1768, to the preſident and council of Bengal; the directors ordered, that the dead ſtock, conſiſting of forts, buildings, and works, and their appurtenances, ſhould have no place in the quick ſtock.

And your Committee find, that in the annual account of 1769, the amount of fortifications, &c. was again added under the head of factory at Bengal, by order of the court of directors, in the manner before mentioned: and that the court of directors have continued to add the ſaid amount, and all additional charges for fortifications, buildings, &c. in all their annual accounts made up ſince that period.

Your Committee have annexed the account which was laid before them relative to the above matters.

And your Committee find by an account delivered to them, and which is hereunto annexed, that the company have expended in fortifications, buildings, &c. at Bengal, from May 1757 ——	2,313,849
And at Fort St. George, from May 1761	596,747
And at Bombay from August 1760	760,551
And at Bencoolen, from July 1761	29,277
And at St. Helena, from October 1761	28,128
	£.3,728,552

Your Committee having now, in pursuance of the order of the house, reported a state of the debts, credits, and effects, of the said company in England and abroad; they are proceeding, pursuant to another part of the said order, to enquire into the situation of the company's affairs; and in the first place, with respect to the profits which the company derive from their commerce, or from the territorial acquisitions lately obtained in the East Indies; an examination of which is necessary, in order to form a competent judgment of the state of the company's affairs.—They have already made some progress in this enquiry; and they will report from time to time, what they find material on this important subject.

A.

To the Right Honourable the Lords Commiſſioners of his Majeſty's Treaſury.

The Memorial of the Court of Directors of the United Company of Merchants of England, trading to the Eaſt-Indies,

Humbly Sheweth,

THAT the prompt payment for the goods ſold by the ſaid Company in their ſale which commenced the 10th of March laſt, having of unavoidable neceſſity been deferred to a late day, the Company are thereby deprived of the receipt of a ſeaſonable and ſufficient ſupply of money to diſcharge the unrated cuſtoms which became due to the crown the 5th of this inſtant Auguſt amounting to about the ſum of £.203,619. 7s. 7d.

Your Memorialiſts therefore moſt humbly pray your Lordſhips will be favourably pleaſed to extend the time for payment of the ſaid £.203,619. 7s. 7d. for two months from the ſaid 5th of Auguſt.

Signed by order of the ſaid Court of Directors.

Eaſt-India Houſe,
the 7th of Auguſt, 1772.

P. Michell, Secretary.

After our hearty commendations. Having conſidered the annexed Memorial of the Court of Directors

Directors of the United Company of Merchants trading to the East-Indies, praying a respite of payment of two hundred and three thousand six hundred and nineteen pounds, seven shillings, and seven pence, or thereabouts, which was due for duties on teas on the 5th of August instant, these are to authorize and require you to cause process to be stayed against the said Company for the said duties, until the 1st day of October 1772, upon their paying interest at the rate of six per cent. for the monies so retained, according to an act of the 4th year of Queen Anne, Chap. 6. And for so doing this shall be your Warrant. Whitehall Treasury Chambers, the 13th day of August 1772.

To our very loving Friends, the Commissioners of his Majesty's Customs, and the Commissioners of his Majesty's excise, and to all other persons whom it may concern.

North.
J. Dyson.
C. Townshend.

East-India Company. Payment of duties on their teas to be respited for two months from 5th August 1762.

To

B.

To the Right honourable the Lords Commiſſioners of his Majeſty's Treaſury.

The Memorial of the Court of Directors of the United Company of Merchants of England, trading to the Eaſt-Indies,

Sheweth,

THAT your Lordſhips were pleaſed on your Memorialiſts application, dated the 7th of Auguſt laſt, to prolong until the 1ſt of October next, the payment of the ſum of £.203,619. 7s. 7d. which became due to the crown the 5th of the ſame month of Auguſt, for the Cuſtoms on unrated goods ſold in their ſale which commenced the 10th of March laſt.

That your Memorialiſts not having received any aid of caſh from the goods ſold in their preſent September ſale, occaſioned by the general ſcarcity of money; and that the ſale of your Memorialiſts Bengal piece goods being unavoidably poſtponed until the enſuing month of November, they are deprived of the means of providing a ſupply for the diſcharge of the ſaid ſum of £.203,619. 7s. 7d. on the 1ſt of October next.

Your Memorialiſts therefore humbly beſeech your Lordſhips will be favourably pleaſed to extend the term for payment of the ſaid ſum of £.203,619. 7s. 7d. for two months from the ſaid 1ſt of October next.

Signed by order of the ſaid Court of Directors.
East-India Houſe, the
24th September 1772.

P. Michell, Secretary.

After

After our hearty commendations. Having confidered the annexed Memorial of the Court of Directors of the United Company of Merchants, trading to the Eaft-Indies, praying a refpite of payment of two hundred and three thoufand fix hundred and nineteen pounds, feven fhillings, and feven pence, or thereabouts, which was due for Cuftoms on unrated goods upon the 5th day of Auguft laft, thefe are to authorize and require you to caufe procefs to be ftayed againft the faid Company for the faid duties, for the fpace of two months, to be computed from the 1ft day of October next, upon their paying intereft after the rate of £.6 per cent. for the monies fo retained, according to an act of the 4th year of the reign of Queen Anne, Chap. 6. And for fo doing this fhall be your Warrant. Whitehall Treafury Chambers, the 30th Sept. 1772.

To our very loving Friends the Commiffioners of his Majefty's Cuftoms.

North.
C. Jenkinfon.
J. Dyfon.

Eaft-India Company. Payment of duties on unrated goods to be refpited for two months from 1 October 1772.

C.

To the Right honourable the Lords Commissioners of his Majesty's Treasury.

The Memorial of the Court of Directors of the United Company of Merchants of England trading to the East-Indies,

Sheweth,

THAT your Lordships were favourably pleased on your Memorialists application, dated the 7th August last, to prolong until the 1st of October last, the payment of the sum of £.203,619. 7s. 7d. which became due to the crown the 5th of the said month of August, for the Customs on unrated goods sold in their sale which commenced the 10th of March last; and that your Lordships were also further pleased to grant further respite of the payment of the said sum of £.203,619. 7s. 7d. until the 1st day of December next.

That the sale of your Memorialists Bengal piece goods not being yet finished, your Memorialists are still disabled from providing a sufficiency of cash for the payment of the said sum of £.203,619. 7s. 7d. on the said 1st day of December next.

Your Memorialists therefore humbly request your Lordships will be pleased to extend the term for payment of the said sum of £.203,619. 7s. 7d. for two months from the 1st day of December next.

Signed by order of the said Court of Directors.

East-India House, the
24th of Nov. 1772.

P. Michell, Secretary.

After

After our hearty commendations. Having considered the annexed Memorial of the Court of Directors of the United Company of Merchants trading to the East-Indies, praying a respite of payment of two hundred and three thousand six hundred and nineteen pounds, seven shillings, and seven pence, or thereabouts, which was due for Customs on unrated goods, upon the 5th of August last, these are to authorize and require you to cause process to be stayed against the said Company, for the said duties, till Wednesday the 9th day of December next, upon their paying interest at the rate of £.6. per cent. for the monies so retained, according to an act of the 4th year of the reign of Queen Anne, Chap. 6. And for so doing this shall be your Warrant. Whitehall Treasury Chambers, the 30th day of November 1772.

To our very loving Friends, the Commissioners of his Majesty's Customs.

C. Jenkinson.
J. Dyson.
C. Townshend.

East-India Company. Payment of duties on unrated goods to be respited till 9th December 1772.

D.

An Account of the Debts of the Eaſt-India Company, bearing Intereſt (excluſive of Bond Debts) the 1ſt day of December 1772, expreſſing the Rate of Intereſt each Debt bears.

	£.	s.	d.	
Amount of the old bullion debt due to the Bank of England—	£. 200,000	0	0	bearing Int. at the Rate of 4 per cent. per Ann.
Amount of what due to the Bank of England upon Loan——	500,000	0	0	Ditto — Ditto— 4 Ditto
Amount of what due to the government for indemnity on tea	202,156	10	0	Ditto — Ditto—12 Ditto
Amount of what due to government as per agreement ——	200,000	0	0	Ditto — Ditto—15 Ditto
Amount of what due to the government for unrated cuſtoms—	203,619	7	7	Ditto — Ditto— 6 Ditto
Amount of bills of exchange —— —— —	699,888	8	10	Ditto — Ditto— 3 Ditto
Amount of what due for freight and demorage —— ——	80,000	0	0	Ditto — Ditto— 4 Ditto
Amount for the fund of Alms-houſes at Poplar — — ——	8,313	16	0	Ditto — Ditto— 4 Ditto
	£. 2,093,978	2	5	

London, the 1ſt *December* 1772.

Errors excepted.

R. Tookey, Dept. Accompt.

E.

Extract of the Letter from the Nabob of Arcot to the Court of Directors, dated the 20th March, 1772.

EVERY demand hitherto made on me by your Governor and Council, I have fully paid, though I could not prevail on them to give me my accounts till very lately, and even those are wrote in such a manner, that neither I nor any of my people can well understand them: However, from the beginning of my transactions to the end of October, 1771, there is not a daum due from me to the Company. The Governor and Council, in December, 1769, thought proper to charge to my account ten lacks of pagodas, as my share of the expence of the Mysore war; they have frequently mentioned in their letters to me, that I acknowledged this as a just debt, and promised to pay it; and I understand from your letters, that they had been at great pains to write in the same manner to England: In the Mysore war I expended large sums, as I maintained the whole army, paid the expence of the troops, as well those employed in the war, as in the defence of the Carnatick at the time: By what management then could the extraordinary expences amount to such a sum? This is the sense I have always had of the agreement I entered into with the Governor and Council in 1768, that I was to be put in possession of the conquered country, out of the revenues of which the whole expence of the war was to have been paid. The event of the war is well known, and in every one article the Governor and Council failed on their part, even in such as I esteemed essential to my honour, as well as to

my

my intereſt, and that of my country. I deſire you to conſider this matter well, and am certain, that you will then ſee this matter in the light I do; and I appeal to yourſelves, whether you think it probable I ever could be brought voluntarily to acknowledge this demand as a juſt debt in ſuch circumſtances.

I have nothing ſo much at heart as endeavouring by every means to make my friendſhip with the Company ſtronger and ſtronger; and therefore, in my laſt letter by the ſhip Lord North, I told you, that the next ſhip ſhould bring you accounts of my friendſhip, that you might ſet your minds at eaſe. What is money to me without your friendſhip? or what ſum can equal the value I have for you? Therefore, ſince you have been told, that I would pay you ten lacks of pagodas, I now tell you, that, out of pure friendſhip, and merely as the reſult of my own free will and choice, I will, in time of peace and tranquility, pay to my friends the Eaſt-India Company ten lacks of pagodas: I aſk nothing in return but your friendſhip, which I doubt not but you will readily grant.

F

ANNUAL ACCOUNT, 1765.

Fort William Quick Stock, dated the 26th November, 1764.

It is the opinion of the Committee of Accounts, That there be deducted from the balance of the above quick ſtock account, for the reaſons mentioned in the engineers letters from Bengal of the 26th

26th November and 1ſt December, 1764, both received per Devonſhire the 15th June, 1765, £ 300,000

ANNUAL ACCOUNT, 1766.

Fort William Quick Stock, dated the 11th March, 1765, and received per Bute the 15th January, 1766.

It is the opinion of the Chairman and Deputy Chairman, That there ſhould be deducted from the balance of the above quick ſtock account, for the reaſons mentioned in the engineers letters from Bengal, dated the 26th November and 1ſt December, 1764, both received per Devonſhire the 15th June, 1765 —— —— £ 330,000

ANNUAL ACCOUNT, 1767.

Fort William Quick Stock, dated the 28th November, 1766, and received per Cruttenden the 19th June, 1767.

Ordered by the Committee of Accounts, That the ſame amount as was deducted from the balance of the laſt year's quick ſtock account, be for the ſame reaſons deducted from the above quick ſtock account —— —— 330,000

The Committee are alſo of opinion, That the ſum of 251,297 l. being the remaining charge for fortifications and buildings in the above quick ſtock account, ſhould likewiſe be deducted; a memorandum of which ſtands at the foot of the annual account, but the ſame was not deducted.

A N-

ANNUAL ACCOUNT, 1768.

Fort William Quick Stock, dated the 10th December, 1767, and received per Norfolk the 12th June, 1768.

Ordered by the Committee of Accounts, That all the charges for buildings, &c. (as per account received from the Auditor) be deducted from the balance of the above quick ſtock account, amounting to — — £ 860,065

ANNUAL ACCOUNT, 1769.

Fort William Quick Stock, dated the 18th November, 1768, and received per Verelſt the 28th May, 1769.

By order of Court, the 27th April, 1769, the ſum of 853,920 l. part of what was deducted from the laſt year's balance of quick ſtock, is added to the above quick ſtock account, not being included therein — — — £ 853,920

ANNUAL ACCOUNT, 1770.

Fort William Quick Stock, dated the 23d November, 1769, and received per Hampſhire the 17th April, 1770.

Per order of Court, the 27th April, 1769, the ſum of 853,920 l. part of what was deducted from the quick ſtock, in the annual account of 1768, is added to the above quick ſtock account, not being included therein - £ 853,920

Brought

Brought forward ———	853,920
Ordered by the Committee of Accounts, That what was expended on fortifications, &c. ſince making up the annual account in 1769, be alſo added to the above quick ſtock account (as per account received from Mr. Hoole) is ——— ——— —	85,880
	£939,800

ANNUAL ACCOUNT, 1771.

The ſum of 853,920 l. having been deducted for fortifications, buildings, &c. from the Bengal quick ſtock, in the annual account of June, 1768, and being omitted in the above quick ſtock, is here added to the preſent balance, per order of Court, the 27th April, 1769 ——— ———	£ 853,920
The 28th June, 1770, the Committee of Accounts ordered, That the increaſed amount on the expence of fortifications and buildings, which appeared by the accounts received from Bengal, ſince making up the annual ſtatement in June, 1769, ſhould be alſo added to this account, as per minute received from the Auditor ——— ———	£ 85,880
The 25th June, 1771, the Committee of Accounts ordered, That the increaſed amount on the expence of fortifications and buildings, which appeared by the accounts received from Bengal, ſince making up the annual ſtatement in June, 1770, ſhould be alſo added to this account, as per minute received from the Auditor	430,880
	£ 1,370,680

ANNUAL ACCOUNT, 1772.

	£.
The ſum of £.853,920. having been deducted for fortifications, buildings, &c. from the Bengal quick ſtock, in the annual account of June 1768, and being omitted in the above quick ſtock, is here added to the preſent balance, per order of Court the 27th April 1769, — —	853,920
The 28th June 1770, the committee of accounts ordered, that the increaſed amount on the expence of fortifications and buildings, which appeared by the accounts received from Bengal, ſince making up the annual ſtatement in June 1769, ſhould be alſo added to this account, as per minute received from the Auditor.—	85,880
The 25th June 1771, the committee of accounts ordered, that the increaſed amount on the expence of fortifications and buildings, which appeared by the accounts received from Bengal, ſince making up the annual ſtatement in June 1770, ſhould be alſo added to this account, as per minute received from the Auditor.—	430,880
The 30th June 1772, the committee of accounts ordered, that the increaſed amount on the expence of fortifications and buildings, which appeared by the accounts received from Bengal, ſince making up the annual ſtatement in June 1771, ſhould be alſo added to this account, as per minute received from the Auditor.—	784,208
	£. 2,154,888

R. Tookey, Deputy Accompt.

AMOUNT of the Sums of Money expended on the Fortifications and Civil Building in the East India Company's Settlements in India, distinguishing each Presidency, to the last Accounts received.

B E N G A L.

Calculate Amount, Buildings, &c. to April 1757 —— —— —— £. st. 187,757

	New Fort. begun 1757-1758.	Dinapore Canton-ments.	Barampore Canton-ments.	Bonkypore Canton-ments.	Mongueer Canton-ments.	Budge Budge Fort.	Total Forts.	Civil Buildings.	
	£. st.	£. st.	£. st.	£. st.	£. st.	£. st.	£. st.	£. st.	
May 1757 to April 1758	51,263	. . . . .	. . . . .	. . . . .	. . . . .	. . . . .	51,263	. . . . .	51,263
1758 1759	141,116	. . . . .	. . . . .	. . . . .	. . . . .	. . . . .	141,116	. . . . .	141,116
1759 1760	84,551	. . . . .	. . . . .	. . . . .	. . . . .	. . . . .	84,551	. . . . .	84,551
1760 1761	14,200	. . . . .	. . . . .	. . . . .	. . . . .	. . . . .	14,200	. . . . .	14,200
1761 1762	31,877	. . . . .	. . . . .	. . . . .	. . . . .	. . . . .	31,877	1,561	33,438
1762 1763	39,181	. . . . .	. . . . .	. . . . .	. . . . .	. . . . .	39,181	1,453	40,634
1763 1764	47,480	. . . . .	. . . . .	. . . . .	. . . . .	. . . . .	47,480	4,288	51,768
1764 1765	42,164	. . . . .	. . . . .	. . . . .	. . . . .	. . . . .	42,164	10,170	52,334
1765 1766	75,563	382	Ef. 13,500	. . . . .	. . . . .	. . . . .	89,445	19,653	109,098
1766 1767	44,103	2,475	D° 27,067	10,962	. . . . .	. . . . .	84,607	15,860	100,407
1767 1768	106,793	43,321	42,830	. . . . .	. . . . .	. . . . .	192,944	29,165	222,109
1768 1769	111,764	68,684	22,657	5,330	6,255	. . . . .	214,688	43,491	258,179
1769 1770	191,374	77,316	47,260	. . . . .	. . . . .	10,417	326,367	23,459	349,826
1770 1771	200,968	48,135	98,530	. . . . .	66	18,422	366,121	18,053	384,174
May 1771 to October 1771	. . . . .	12,115	16,863	. . . . .	. . . . .	27,677	56,655	17,379	74,034
Total carried into the Annual Statement June 1772	1,182,397	252,428	268,707	16,292	6,319	56,516	1,782,659	184,472	2,154,888
Oct. 1771 to March 1772	115,258	. . . . .	34,563	. . . . .	. . . . .	2,858	152,679	6,282	158,961
£. st.	1,297,655	252,428	302,270	16,292	6,319	59,374	1,935,338	190,754	2,313,840

Bombay.

Calculate Amount, Buildings, &c. to July 1760. — —

	Bombay Fort.	Glacis and cover'd way round Town Ditch.	Fortifications Dungaree Hill.	Dock and Pier Battery.	New Barracks.	Castle at Surat.
	£. st.	£. st.	£. st.	£. st.	£. st.	£. st.
August 1760 to July 1761	12,302	6,388	2,993	8,726	8,056	1,770
1761 1762	1,940	827	59	808	2,986	716
1762 1763	16,771	11,363	29	3,301	318	. . . . .
1763 1764	8,901	374	2,141	982	836	663
1764 1765	9,362	26	. . . . .	1,159	. . . . .	1,415
1765 1766	11,008	3,137	. . . . .	2,196	1,228	463
1766 1767	7,738	17,007	. . . . .	2,445	52	1,679
1767 1768	3,706	21,397	. . . . .	2,451	. . . . .	2,693
1768 1769	2,768	20,744	12,799	1,215	. . . . .	1,502
1769 1770	16,085	4,411	39,986	1,474	. . . . .	3,943
Total inserted in a Memor. in the Annual Statement, June 1772 — — £. st.	90,601	85,674	58,007	24,757	13,476	14,844

Fort St. George.

Calculate Amount, Buildings, &c. to April 1761 —— —— —— —— £. ft. 334,014

	Madras Fort.	Egmore Redoubt.	Military Barracks.	Masulipatam Fort.	Cuddalore Fort.	Vizagapatam. Fort.	Ganjam Fort.	Black Town Wall.	Total Forts.	Civil Buildings.	
	£. ft.	£. ft.	£. ft.	£. ft.	£. ft.	£. ft.	£. ft.	£. ft.	£. ft.	£. ft.	
lay 1761 to April 1762	. . . . .	. . . . .	. . . . .	. . . . .	. . . . .	. . . . .	. . . . .	. . . . .	. . . . .	. . . . .	. . . . .
1762 1763	. . . . .	. . . . .	. . . . .	. . . . .	. . . . .	. . . . .	. . . . .	. . . . .	. . . . .	. . . . .	. . . . .
1763 1764	. . . . .	. . . . .	. . . . .	. . . . .	. . . . .	. . . . .	. . . . .	. . . . .	. . . . .	. . . . .	. . . . .
1764 1765	15,561	1,934	4,016	. . . . .	. . . . .	. . . . .	. . . . .	. . . . .	21,511	14,605	36,116
1765 1766	18,222	. . . . .	. . . . .	1,744	1,101	. . . . .	. . . . .	. . . . .	21,067	1,296	22,363
1766 1767	14,186	. . . . .	. . . . .	5,809	7,694	251	. . . . .	. . . . .	27,940	4,425	32,365
1767 1768	18,866	. . . . .	. . . . .	5,909	1,384	11	. . . . .	. . . . .	26,170	3,466	29,636
1768 1769	20,351	. . . . .	. . . . .	4,968	1,412	288	. . . . .	. . . . .	27,019	3,473	30,492
1769 1770	13,485	3,436	. . . . .	7,981	430	9	3,534	. . . . .	28,875	214	29,089
otal inserted in a Memor. in the Annual Statement June 1772	100,671	5,370	4,016	26,411	12,021	559	3,534	. . . . .	152,582	27,479	514,075
1770 —— 1771	15,651	. . . . .	. . . . .	10,883	647	1,240	3,570	43,322	75,313	7,359	82,672
£. ft	116,322	5,370	4,016	37,294	12,668	1,799	7,104	43,322	227,895	34,838	596,747

Bencoolen.

Calculate Amount, Buildings, &c. to July 1761 — — — — — £. 9,789

July . . 1761 to Febr. 1762	- - - - -
February 1761 to Oct. 1762	- - - - -
October 1762 to April 1763	749
May . . 1763 to April 1764	4,201
1764 1765	2,648
1765 1766	4,190
1766 1767	1,169
1767 1768	1,434
1768 1769	1,835
1769 1770	3,262

Total inferted in a Memorandum in the Annual Statement, June 1772. — £. ft. 29,277

Saint Helena.

Calculate Amount, Buildings, &c. to 1761 - - - - - - - - - - -	£.19,920
October 1761 to September 1762 - - - - - - - - - - -	
1762 - - - - 1763 - - - - - - - - - - -	
1763 - - - - 1764 - - - - - - - - - - -	
1764 - - - - 1765 - - - - - - - - - - -	
1765 - - - - 1766 - - - - - - - - - - -	
1766 - - - - 1767 - - - - - - - - - - -	
1767 - - - - 1768 - - - - - - - - - - -	
1768 - - - - 1769 - - - - - - - - - - -	
1769 - - - - 1770 - - - - - - - - - - -	
1770 - - - - 1771 - - - - - - - - -	8,208
Total inserted in a Memorandum in the Annual Statement, June 1772	£. st. 28,128

East-India House,
10th December 1772.

Errors excepted.

John Hoole,
Auditor of Indian Accounts.

www.ingramcontent.com/pod-product-compliance
Lightning Source LLC
Chambersburg PA
CBHW021533270326
41930CB00008B/1233
* 9 7 8 3 3 3 7 1 5 0 4 5 7 *